The High-Octane Church
7 Principles for Vibrant Church Growth

by

JACQUES FRANÇOIS

Table of Contents

Introduction	Software Upgrade	i
Chapter 1	The Buck Stops Here!	1
Chapter 2	But Why?	9
Chapter 3	Bring Back The Romance!	15
Chapter 4	No More Sparklers!	23
Chapter 5	Just Like Your Daddy	33
Chapter 6	All Hands On Deck	41
Chapter 7	What's Mine Is Yours	49
Chapter 8	What They Don't Say	55
Chapter 9	Value Added	59
	About The Author	63

INTRODUCTION

Software Upgrade

From time to time I receive notifications that there are updates available for various apps on my smartphone. Most of the time, the update entails bug fixes, performance enhancements, or some minor aesthetic change. On rare occasions, the update screams for a new version. The app goes through massive alterations and when this type of update finishe taking shape, the app looks, performs, and feels different. Options not available in the previous version, surfaces in the new adaptation. The new version functions more efficiently and effortlessly. God upgraded the software of the Old Testament church and takes it through a metamorphosis in the New Testament. Christ, through His death, employed a new version of the church. It was pertinent that God used a new infrastructure to support this software update. The Holy Spirit was the software update and our bodies became the new infrastructure to house this technology that we call the Holy Spirit.

The gospel of Matthew uses the word church for the first time in scripture. *"And I also say to you that you are Peter, and on this rock, I will build My church, and the gates of Hell shall not prevail against it." (Matthew 16:18)* The word church comes from the Greek word ekklēsia, and it means the called-out assembly. **"But ye are a chosen generation, a royal priesthood, a holy nation, a peculiar people; that he should show forth the praises of Him who called you out of darkness into His marvelous light." (1 Peter 2:9)** The church comprises of people who have been invited out of darkness into His marvelous light. To appreciate this new technology, we have to travel the Bible's time machine back to the Old Testament. Exodus 25:8 says: *"And let them make Me a sanctuary, that I may dwell among them."* God's objective is to dwell with His people, and He commanded Moses to have the people build a structure so that God could live among His people in a prominent, physical, and personal way. The omnipresent God confined Himself to a tent, which was the first version of the earthly sanctuary. Because the children of Israel were vagabonds in the wilderness, they needed an edifice that was flexible enough to move when God indicated that it was time to set up camp elsewhere. The second version was built by King Solomon, and it was a permanent fixture in Jerusalem because Israel were no longer nomads but were stationary with borders to protect. The sanctuary became the center of the spiritual life of God's people. The people went to the temple to sacrifice, to the temple to worship, and to the temple to receive religious instruction. The temple was at the heart of the plan of salvation. This version of the church was not flexible enough to have an astronomical influence on the world. In many cases, a non-Jew would have to take a pilgrimage from his or her country, like the Queen of Sheba, to be influenced by what was centered at the temple.

Jesus uses the word ekklēsia and it does not indicate a

stationary building, but a living organism. Brick and mortar do not define the church, but people. We call our church buildings a name, but God called people by name to be His church. God uniquely rolled out His upgrade. **"What? Know ye not that your body is the temple of the Holy Ghost, which is in you, which ye have of God, and ye are not your own?" (1 Corinthians 6:19)** We possess the indwelling power of the Holy Spirit. In us, God has a sanctuary, and He reconstructs us to house the presence of God. Now the temple is once again portable. Wherever you and I reside, there the church resides. When we move the church moves, and where we go, according to the commission, the church goes as well. No one has to commute to the church any longer, the church can now go wherever the lost are. The high-octane church can go to the countryside, mountainside, seaside, to every desert, jungle, village, town, and metropolitan city in the world. Our three-fold commission, to go to all nations, becomes a reality because of the innovation of God.

Anti-Virus

In the New Testament, God installed a new version of the church software which came with an anti-virus package. Part b of Matthew 16:18 says, "and the gates of hell shall not prevail against it." Satan has been trying for years to hack the church, but God immunized her against such malicious attacks. What does Jesus mean when He says the gates of hell will not prevail against the church? The word hell comes from the Greek word *hades*. It means death or the grave. Please don't miss this. Death cannot infect the church and shut down the operating system. If thoughts of closing the church you are shepherding dominate your mind, recognize God did not design the church to die. Men and women close church doors, not God. God promised that death cannot stage a coup against the church. We are alive with Christ *(Ephesians 2:5)*. As long as we are alive, the church is alive.

Human Error

Jesus said in Matthew 16:18: *"And I also say to you that you are Peter, and on this rock, I will build My church, and the gates of Hades shall not prevail against it."* There are some great church models that can be used to grow the church and expand the kingdom of God. Something the church has to find a way to grapple with is that almost all church models are in some way pastor focused. At times, it is very difficult to differentiate the line between pastoral leadership and ministries revolving around the pastor. Throughout biblical history we do see models where God used the charisma of single individuals, especially in the Old Testament. We have the Moses model of leadership, where Moses climbs the mountain, receives instruction from God, and then returns to tell the people what God said. Later in Israel's history we see an elaborate system where God worked through potentates; He established the house of David to dominate the throne until Jesus came. God worked through priests; He established the house of Aaron to intercede at the altar until Jesus becomes our High Priest. God spoke through prophets *(Elijah)* who at times were the main medium of communication between God and His people, until God speaks prophetically through Jesus *(Hebrews 1:1)*. There were also individuals who were raised up to preside over the people as judges and act as their champions to deliver them from the tyranny of heathen oppression *(Samson)*. Now Christ functions as our champion in that He has delivered us from the grip of sin and the sting of death. When we get to the New Testament, God uses a slightly different model. The church belongs to Jesus Christ and He serves as the dominant figure in the church, and instead of centering the church on the skill set of one main individual, Christ serves as a general contractor and we serve as subcontractors. A general contractor's goal is to build a building. According to the text, Jesus is concerned with building a church. The general contractor does not pour the foundation, build the frame, or install electrical wiring and plumbing – He/she hires subcontractors. Jesus uses the same approach. According to Ephesians 4:11-12, **"And He Himself gave some to be apostles, some prophets, some evangelists, and some pastors and teachers, for the equipping of the saints for the work of ministry, for the edifying of the body of Christ."** Notice, the church is supposed to be equipped and edified. Equipping is preparing, and edifying is building up. God dispatches spiritual gifts so that the church can be trained to do ministry and build up the church. We partner with God to build the church He desires.

One thing that contributes to the church failing to function as a high-octane church is that the leadership does not always focus on equipping the people to build up the church. Instead, pastors and ministry leaders are content with doing all the work, and everyone else serving as assistants. We have to invite everyone who sits in the pew to jump into the trenches with us. God needs all hands-on-deck. In the following chapters of this book, we will focus on what I call the seven P's that I believe must be present in every church in order for it to be a high-octane church. These seven P's are located in the first and second chapters of Acts and when all seven P's are activated, the scripture gives the results of what happened: **"And the Lord added to the church daily such as should be saved." (Acts 2:47b)**

This book is an invitation for you to voyage with me. God convicted me that through His power our churches can be magnetized by the Holy Spirit with an influx of people being added to the church daily. Let us not give up and hammer the nail into the coffin. Hold off on the funeral service of our churches. Rather, allow Jesus to raise our dying churches like He raised Lazarus and make it a living organism that cannot die but multiply.

> **There exists a church growth epidemic in America and its contagion has gripped the world.**

CHAPTER 1

The Buck Stops Here!

The pressure to grow churches has escalated to an unsustainable apex, driven ministry leaders to breaking points, sabotaged divine potential, crushed energetic ambitions, and endorsed ministries that thrive but may not be anointed by the Holy Spirit. There exists a church growth epidemic in America and its contagion has gripped the world. The subject of Church growth deluge ministry leaders with books, conferences, seminars, webinars, blogs, programs, and the list goes on and on. Products saturate bookstores, the online space, and feed our insatiable desire to grow the next big church. I believe every effort to grow and expand the kingdom of God is well-intentioned and mandated by the God of this universe, but shortcuts have created a plethora of churches who use the wrong metrics to measure the fulfillment of the gospel commission. When we witness churches explode in numerical growth, the desire to grow our own ministry or church compels us to mimic an entire system that may not flourish in our context. I am not insinuating that we should not learn from each other. There are basic attributes every church should have in common but neglecting to allow God to personally shape your ministry teeters towards catastrophe.

We chase with desperation the blueprint of other ministries and rarely pursue the prototype that God gave to His people. At the very least, God's masterplan ignites high-octane churches! Matthew 16:18 (NKJV) says: *"And I also say to you that you are Peter, and on this rock I will build My church, and the gates of Hades shall not prevail against it."* The word church comes from the Greek word ekklēsia. It means the called-out assembly. God called the Church. The church is appointed. God builds His called-out assembly upon a bedrock (*Petra*), which is the truth of Christ's messiahship and sonship. God imbues the church, not with failure, but with the prospect of experiencing astronomical multiplication through His power and might. The expansion is two-fold. God designed the church to first multiply spiritually and second numerically, and both are supposed to happen simultaneously. God yearns for everyone to come to repentance (*2 Peter 3:9*). The church drives the vehicle of salvation. The church proclaims the mandates of the gospel. The church serves as watchmen on the wall who cry aloud and spare not.

When the great divine Architect drafted the masterplan of the church, He established her as the greatest institution on earth. The church is the 'apple of His eye' (Zechariah 2:8). The Church is considered the bride of Christ. "Husbands, love your wives, just as Christ also loved the church and gave Himself for her, that He might sanctify and cleanse her with the washing of water by the word, that He might present her to Himself a glorious church, not having spot or wrinkle or any such thing, but that she should be holy and without blemish" (Ephesians 5:25-27). God loves His church so much that He allowed His own demise on her behalf and He craves to make her a glorious church. God empowers her with the potency of heaven. He gives her His Holy Spirit. Keep in mind that God immunizes the church from the conquering forces of the evil one. It does not matter how large or small your church is. It does not matter the geographical location. It does not matter the cultural or social issues that dominate the community in which you minister. Every church can be and should be a high-octane church.

What does a high-octane church look like? We have to look at this question three ways to really answer the question. Acts 2:47 sets the stage for what we consider high-octane. The scripture says: "And the Lord added to the church daily those who were being saved."

And The Lord Added To The Church

Conflict cripple churches. Internal fighting? Yes! The apostle Paul addressed an issue that arose in the church at Corinth. In his first letter to the Corinthians, Paul speaks to the carnality that epitomized the church and festered into open combat. Those who were in Apollos' camp contended against those who were in the camp of Paul, and vice-versa. Paul says in verses 3 and 4 of 1 Corinthians chapter 3, *"For ye are yet carnal: for whereas there is among you envying, and strife, and divisions, are ye not carnal, and walk as men? For while one says, I am of Paul; and another, I am of Apollos; are ye not carnal?"* Notice how Paul classifies this tension as unspiritual, because the trepidations contradict the purpose of the respective ministries of Paul and Apollos. He then offers them the true reason why the church existed. In verses 5 and 6 he says: "Who then is Paul, and who is Apollos, but ministers by whom ye believed, even as the Lord gave to every man? I have planted, Apollos watered; but God gave the increase." Obviously, God takes the credit for the increase that took place in Corinth. When we attribute church growth to someone's elaborate plan, we create a paradoxical impasse that fails to foster unity, and forces everyone into opposing camps. Unfortunately, no one ends up in the camp of Christ. Each member of the Corinthian fellowship, no matter whose preaching or teaching they heard, were all considered God's increase.

God's machine of salvation should overwhelm us of the notion that we labor and nothing more, and all the glory belongs to God. God expands the church. God adds to her fellowship. We can plant seeds in the most fertile soil and use the highest quality H2O to nourish the seed, but if the Son of Righteousness does not initiate divine photosynthesis, nothing will grow, and there will not be a harvest of souls. It has always been God's plan to increase the church. Our only calling entails working within the constraints of His sacred model.

And The Lord Added To The Church Daily

Here, idealism on my part begins to take shape, because complacency overrides the efficiency of the church. Church usually consists of a weekend program and maybe one program during the week. People normally see church as a building. Church is a place I go to, instead of church being something I am. Church is not an event. You and I embody the church. Wherever you and I exist, there exists the church. Remember, church consists of people who have been 'called out of darkness into His marvelous light *(1 Peter 2:9)*'. According to Acts 2:47, the Lord added to the church daily. In order to supplement the pews with new people, the church functioned every day. Does this mean that there was a church service every day? Maybe or maybe not. At the very least, it means that the people who made up the church operated in a way that salvation of new converts was accomplished even while the church building was silent.

How many people can say that the fellowship they belong to is growing numerically every day? The preaching of the gospel was a daily phenomenon. It was not relegated to a weekend, quarterly, or yearly event and more people than the preacher presented it. The gospel dominated the circadian routine of the early church. "And daily in the temple, and in every house, they ceased not to teach and preach Jesus Christ (Acts 5:42)." The gospel infiltrated the community surrounding the individuals that characterized the church. The members relentlessly broadcasted the good news of Jesus Christ. Jesus said of Himself, *"And I, if I be lifted up from the earth, will draw all men unto me (John 12:32)."* They put Christ on the cross every day and magnified the great sacrifice He made to secure eternal salvation. Our lovely Savior attracted those who were yet in darkness and lured them into His marvelous light.

And The Lord Added To The Church Daily Those That Were Being Saved

I heard someone say that the church is no longer a hospital, a place where people go to get well, rather it is a hospice, where people go to die. On so many levels I see how it's true. According to the text, the high-octane church is a conglomerate of people who are being saved. God designated the church to be a metropolis where one can run and find refuge from sin and death. The church disintegrates into an obsolete institution if it feeds the belly of the grave with men and women who God marked for salvation.

Salvation in Acts 2:47 comes from the Greek word sōzō (σώζω). This word is in the passive grammatical voice, meaning, salvation happens to us by God. Look where He does it: in the church. Theologically speaking, God can save humanity anywhere. His Godship gives Him full autonomy as He works out our election, but He commissioned the church community to foster the circumstance where this saving act is nurtured for the benefit of each person who is added by God. Please resist the temptation to view the church as a building and therefore envisioning salvation taking place behind the doors of the structural edifice. Keep in mind that the church consists of people. Our salvation takes place in community. In other words, salvation happens to us and people who are being saved are added to us, the church. God adds to the high-octane church and does so in such a potent way that it looks like multiplication, because everyday someone follows Christ to the fellowship. God energizes this society of believers with salvation and the energy is so strong that His saving grace goes viral.

Summary

For the purpose of this book, the definition of a high-octane church is a church where:
- The Lord adds to the church
- The Lord adds to the church daily
- The Lord adds to the church daily those who are being saved

For Your Consideration

Imagine a church where God is literally adding to her ranks on a daily basis. Please consider the following questions. Do I believe that God can ignite this type of growth in my context? What kind of infrastructure would need to be in place for this type of growth? Does my church have this type of infrastructure?

"God equipped us with an ironclad mission, and He gave us the divine clout to accomplish it."

CHAPTER 2

But Why?

During my freshmen year of college there was a young lady who caught my eye. For weeks I tried to manufacture the courage to approach her and introduce myself. I remember that moment like it happened today. I spotted her barreling towards the cafeteria, and I was only a few paces behind her. I picked up my pace and called her name. She stopped and turned around as I approached. She seemed happy to see me, which I took as a good sign. I hesitantly jumped into the speech that I prepared. After some small talk and few laughs, I finally asked her if I could have her number. With a puzzled look she responded, "But why?"

I normally do a good job of not allowing my emotions to paint my face, but I am almost certain that at that moment, a look of awkward confusion possessed me. I responded, "Because I would like to talk to you more often."

Like a broken record, she asked a second time, "But why?" At this moment I am picking my face off the ground. I was not sure if she was testing me or if she genuinely wanted to know. I responded, "because I would like to get to know you better." She responded again, "But why?"

But Why?

I was unable to articulate my why and therefore I failed to convince her that she should buy into my mission to get to know her better. The high-octane church has virtuous intentions, but too often the church fails to assert its why. The why clearly and succinctly verbalizes the mission. Thankfully, Jesus did the heavy lifting of defining the church's why. He gave us the high-octane commission in three parts, and neither can survive apart from the others; they interconnect. All three parts of the commission finds fulfillment only if they inundate the entire globe, together. In other words, the church cannot quarantine her commission to the local community. Yes, she starts with her immediate context, but she must spread her wings over the entire world. **"But you shall receive power when the Holy Spirit has come upon you; and you shall be witnesses to Me in Jerusalem, and in all Judea and Samaria, and to the end of the earth." Acts 1:8.** The why of any organization is normally answered by the contents of the mission. Jesus answers the why in the commission.

Commission Part 1 – Mark 16:15-16

"And he said unto them, go ye into all the world, and preach the gospel to every creature. He that believeth and is baptized shall be saved; but he that believeth not shall be damned." The first part of our mission is to go into all the world and preach the gospel, the good news of Jesus Christ. I must stress that preaching and teaching are two different endeavors. The Greek word for preach is *kēryssō* (κηρύσσω). It means to cry out loud. The gospel rumbles from the lips of the preacher and escalates into an earthquake and violently shakes the world.

Commission Part 2 – Luke 24:46-47

"And said unto them, thus it is written, and thus it behooved Christ to suffer, and to rise from the dead the third day: And that repentance and remission of sins should be preached in His name among all nations, beginning at Jerusalem." Repentance comes from the Greek word metanoia (μετάνοια). It means a changed mind and changed direction. Remission comes from the Greek word aphesis (ἄφεσις). It means pardon. In other words, the second part of our mission is to preach to change minds, inspire people to turn away from their sins, and accept the pardon that God offers through Jesus Christ.

Commission Part 3 – Matthew 28:19-20

"Go therefore and make disciples of all the nations, baptizing them in the name of the Father and of the Son and of the Holy Spirit, teaching them to observe all things that I have commanded you; and lo, I am with you always, even to the end of the age. Amen." The Greek word for disciple is a powerful word. We normally think of a disciple as one who follows Christ or one who learns from Him. The role of the disciple is more thorough. The word mathēteuō (μαθητεύω) identifies a person who awakens to be committed to Christ. *Didaskō*, teaching, according to verse 20 awakens this commitment. I must pause at this juncture, because we have accepted a complacent spirit when it comes to this topic. Most churches do not have a developed discipleship program. Inactive members litter our church roles. We have many members who show up only during Easter weekend. In many cases, we are diligent about the preached word and not about the taught word. To push the point further, we must not teach

just for the sake of disseminating information. Rather, we teach to awaken the people's commitment to Christ. The church is the only institution on earth that promotes a lifestyle after the similitude of Jesus Christ.

The high-octane church exists to preach the gospel to all the world, preach repentance and remission from sin among all nations, and make disciples of all nations by teaching men and women to observe everything Christ commanded.

The Acts Model

In the second chapter of Acts we see how the three-part commission was activated on the day of Pentecost. The Holy Spirit filled the 120 individuals who assembled in the upper chamber. They began to speak in tongues to the multitude who assembled from other nations in Jerusalem. Verses 8-11 lists all the various nations that were represented in Jerusalem. The gospel of Jesus Christ was dynamically preached. Verse 11 says: "We do hear them speak in our tongues the wonderful works of God (gospel – *commission part 1*)." In verses 37 and 38: "Now when they heard this, they were pricked in their heart, and said unto Peter and to the rest of the apostles, Men and brethren, what shall we do? Then Peter said unto them, *repent (commission part 2,* and be baptized *(commission part 3)* every one of you in the name of Jesus Christ for the *remission of sins*, and ye shall receive the gift of the Holy Ghost." In verse 42: "And they continued steadfastly in the apostles' doctrine *(teaching – commission part 3)* and fellowship, and breaking of bread, and in prayers." We see the climax in Acts 2:47, "Praising God and having favor with all the people. And the Lord added to the church daily those who were being saved." The three-fold mission ran through the blood of the early church.

The Mission Vs. Commission

Traditionally, we have referred to Matthew 28:18-20 as the great commission, but as we have seen, that has to be expanded to a three-dimensional commission. We must talk about the word commission for a bit. When one reads any of the three scriptural references that identifies our why, the word commission is not used in any of the contexts. If we claim that we have a commission, we must understand that it is different from a mission. A mission answers why an organization exists. Commission, on the other hand, is defined as the act of granting *power* or *authority* to carry out a particular task or duty. Jesus said in Matthew 28:18, "all authority has been given to Me in heaven and on earth." We not only received purpose from Christ, but we also received potency from Christ. He not only gave us our assignment, but through the commission He gave us the authority to carry it out. This is revolutionary because impotence cannot set the tone of the church any longer. God equipped us with an ironclad mission, and He gave us the divine clout to accomplish it. The high-octane church has a compelling why. Christ not only told us to focus on three main things, but He gave us the force we need to make them a reality. The commission is bigger than our realities, it is inspirational because God asked us to do something that is unattainable in our own strength, but the possibilities are vast because Jesus Himself will give us what we need to accomplish it.

The 1st 'P' Of A High-Octane Church Is Purpose

- What is it about the commission that supersedes any mission statement an organization can craft?

> **Prayer has fallen from grace in the eyes of the church and it is the least erotic thing that the church does.**

CHAPTER 3

Bring Back The Romance!

On various occasions my wife has reminded me that I do not write letters to her, nor pen words of poetry like I regularly did while we were dating. She reminisces about the times I surprised her with rose petals and cards. She talks about the walks we took in the park and when we spent time on the phone till the wee hours of the morning. She transports my recollection to the moments that I trusted her with my innermost secrets. We did not have a care in the world. Without being obnoxious and blunt, obviously her soul screams to me: bring back the romance! Romance keeps the fire burning in relationships, it draws out the best in each individual, and it guards against insecure feelings. Romantic activities communicate to the love of your life that you are still acutely in-tuned to the essence of their souls. I have noticed that when I am aggressively letting my wife know that she is the most important thing to me in the world, there is nothing she will not do for me.

When the wedding bells rang and Christ vowed to love us in sickness and in health, ecstatic emotions ran rampant as Christ made the church His bride. After the high of being in a saving relationship with God waned, the fire and the passion began to disintegrate into a flickering flame. God savors the moments when we talked to Him all night long and He remembers when we gave Him the flowers of our prayers. He is now longing for His bride to bring back the romance! Obviously, if there is a lack of communication in any relationship, the relationship will decompose. If absent discourse between God and His bride defines the talking points, if our souls fail to engage God on the hotline of heaven, and if prayer evaporates from our souls, the connection with God will cease to exist.

The 2nd 'P' Of A High-Octane Church Is Prayer

Prayer has fallen from grace in the eyes of the church and it is the least erotic thing that the church does. The church engages in more planning than it does praying. In his classic book *The Complete Works of E.M.* Bounds, brother Bounds relates the importance of prayer when he says, "Men are looking for better methods; God is looking for better men (pg. 8)." Prayer is the primary fuel that makes the church combustible. The church cannot run without prayer no more can a car run without gasoline. I am not talking only about the importance of prayer, but the necessity of establishing the prayer assembly.

The high-octane church in the book of Acts understood the urgency of prayer. *"But ye shall receive power, after that the Holy Ghost is come upon you: and ye shall be witnesses unto me both in Jerusalem, and in all Judaea, and in Samaria, and unto the uttermost part of the earth (Acts 1:8)."* The word power in verse 8 is an important word in this discussion. It comes from the Greek word *dynamis*, and it is where we get the word dynamite. Jesus promised the church dynamite in order to carry out her high-octane commission. Notice what the assembly does after Christ gives this promise and ascends into heaven: *"Then returned they unto Jerusalem from the mount called Olivet, which is from Jerusalem a Sabbath day's journey. And when they were come in, they went up into an upper room…, These all continued with one accord in prayer and supplication, with the women, and Mary the mother of Jesus, and with his brethren (Acts 1:12-14)."* Jesus promises perpetual power! The assembly does not wait by listening to the ticks of the clock counting down until Pentecost; No! They hibernated in the upper room and commenced a prayer meeting. For ten days, this group of people who endured the trauma of their Savior being crucified, but renewed with the delight of His resurrection, crammed into the prayer room, zealously supplicating the throne room of heaven, until they heard the sound of the mighty rushing wind, and received the dynamite that came from heaven through the anointing of the Holy Spirit *(Acts 2:2-4)*. Therefore, the prayer chamber became a waiting room where the prayer assembly gathered until the endowment of the Holy Spirit was manifested.

They Were Dedicated

From the inception of the new church that emerged from the day of Pentecost, prayer meetings were the cultural norm of the church. *"And they continued steadfastly in the apostle' doctrine and fellowship, and in breaking of bread, and in prayers (Acts 2:42)."* When the text mentions that they *continued steadfastly*, it means they were devoted to, among other things, prayer. The assembly continuously engaged in prayer. It was no less than what Jesus did during His earthly ministry. Luke 6:12 tells us, "And it came to pass in those days, that He went out into a mountain to pray, and continued all night in prayer to God. If divinity ran through the veins of Christ and He saw the need to pray all night, how much more should we who are mere mortals, susceptible to sin, powerless to resist temptation, and prone to leave the God that we love, engage in ardent prayer sessions.

When Jesus ascended to heaven, He left behind a prayer assembly. Personally, I completely understand why it was vital to do so. Consider the commission Jesus gives them in Matthew 28:19-20; Mark 16:15-16; and Luke 24:46-47. Jesus challenged this meager group of 120 people to go into all the world, without sophisticated forms of transportation, or the novelty of the internet. Going to familiar territory and pursuing the lost sheep of Israel in Matthew 10:5-6 paled in comparison to the fact that they had to venture into unchartered territory. The disciples must have felt overwhelmed at what Christ was asking them to do. Instead of allowing their sense of inadequacy to smother them, they were driven to their knees, understanding that only God could empower them to accomplish such a feat. The commission has not changed, nor the importunity to accomplish it, nor God's need to have militant prayer warriors. Prayer is still the prerequisite of the Holy Spirit perching on our shoulders as He did on the day of Pentecost. There has yet to be a revival or a great awakening, in all the history of humanity, that was not initiated by corporate prayer.

Most ministry leaders in America maintain a robust program to administer the word, but they have a feeble, frail, and flimsy prayer meeting. Some churches have a prayer service during the week, which only a few attend. Others, on the other hand, do not have a prayer service at all. The churches that have a consistent prayer meeting do less praying than they do preaching. This is something that I have encountered in my own pastorate. I found myself trying to pack prayer, testimonies, singing, and preaching into one program. I was always bothered by the fact that we always describe our mid-week service as prayer meeting, but when I tallied the total time that was spent on each segment of the program, approximately 5 minutes was spent engaged in prayer, but I spent 30 minutes, at least, preaching.

The Apostles

In Acts chapter 6, there arose a quarrel in the midst of the called-out assembly because the Hebrew widows were being served more favorably than the Greek widows. To meet this tension head on, the apostles decided to appoint deacons who would take care of the daily ministration. In verse 4, the apostles said, "But we will give ourselves continually to prayer, and the ministry of the word." The passage reads in the original Greek, "But we to *the prayer* and the ministry of the word." I have read this passage many times, and I always assumed the apostles were referring to their own personal prayer life. I was shocked when I realized that the apostles were talking about prayer meeting. The apostles saw their main responsibility consisting of two things; 1) organizing prayer meeting and 2) ministering the word. Most preachers are prolific at ministering the word, but the prayer assembly is in disarray. The dissemination of the word and vibrant prayer assemblies are fraternal twins. Preaching and teaching only, puts us at a disadvantage, because we find ourselves doing all the work, the church becomes dependent on our charisma, and she adopts our personality. When prayer meetings saturate the life of the church, we put the Holy Spirit to work, He dazzles the church with His glamour, and we adopt His sanctified personality, power, and purpose.

Spiritual Warfare

Peter, James, and John descend a high mountain with Jesus after watching Him transfigure in their presence and witnessing Jesus' grand display of glorious affirmation. Once they make their way back down to the foot of the mountain, a man who had a son with a dumb spirit, confronts Jesus with the impotence of His disciples. He explains to Jesus, "And wherever it seizes him, it throws him down; he foams at the mouth, gnashes his teeth, and becomes rigid. So, I spoke to your disciples, that they should cast it out, but they could not." (Mark 9:18) Frustrated at the disciples' incompetence to wage spiritual warfare, Jesus rebuked the unclean spirit. Jesus delivered training and mentorship to these disciples to steward one of His greatest technological advances; the church. Their training wilted in the face of this demonic threat. Obviously embarrassed, the disciples pull Jesus aside privately, and asked Him, "Why could we not cast it out" (Mark 9:28)? Jesus answers in verse 29, that *'This kind can come out by nothing but prayer and fasting.'* In chapter 6, Jesus gave them power over unclean spirits. What happened three chapters later? I will tell you. The disciples neglected the cultivation of their prayer lives. They were ministry driven, there is no question about it, but their ministry did not have the luster it needed, nor the anointing to thrive once thrusted into enemy strongholds. As a result of their sloppy prayer behavior, the disciples experienced defeat and humiliation.

The church battles constantly, but human ingenuity cannot supply her with an arsenal of weapons. "For the weapons of our warfare are not carnal, but mighty through God to the pulling down of strong holds." (2 Corinthians 10:4) We can craft extraordinary mission and vision statements, create exceptional programming, conjure best practices and an impeccable organizational machine, compensate the most experienced and qualified staff, claim that we have the best show in town, and compound our ministry with exponential membership growth, but, only ceaseless combative corporate prayer will act as battle rams to destroy the walls of Jericho and put our churches on the right path to becoming high octane.

Focus On Prayer Meeting

Prayer is not as romantic as praise and worship, preaching, church conferences, church socials, but instituting the prayer meeting is by far the first and most important step in becoming a high-octane church. Honestly speaking, there will be push back from your congregation, church leadership will disparage your efforts, you will become discouraged because initially only a few will show up, and the enemy will work overtime to plant problems in your church that did not previously exist. Put much of your energy into having high-octane prayer meetings; prayer meetings where the only thing that is taking place for a determined time is prayer. Your closet prayer plays a major role in your spiritual development, but corporate prayer plays an enormous role in the church's spiritual development. Teach your people how to pray, preach sermons on the importance of prayer, incorporate collective prayer in the worship services, implement seasons of prayer at staff meetings and any church functions, and take your church on prayer walks in the community. Do not allow anything or anyone to distract you from this most important step. Serenade God with your earnest prayers and bring back the romance!

Bring Back The Romance!

Summary

- The 2nd 'P' of a High-Octane Church is Prayer. Praying for the outpour of the Holy Spirit.

CHAPTER 4

No More Sparklers!

It proved almost impossible for me to contain my elation when the 4th of July rolled in every year. Excitement and apprehension battled in my stomach as I looked forward to the festivities. Excitement; because of the mini explosions caused by smoke balls, bottle rockets, firecrackers, roman candles, artillery shells, and jumping Jacks. Apprehension; because I always hoped that it would be the year that I could graduate from sparklers to the louder bombs that was available in the arsenal of fireworks. Every year, my mother faithfully purchased sparklers, only. When we were young, the sparkler was more than sufficient to quench our thirst for opulence. As we matured, our hearts panted after, what we called, 'real firecrackers.' We begged my mother to upgrade the stockpiles of sparklers she saved every year and give us more variety to choose from. One year she finally relented and purchased us quite a number of cherry bombs. My nephew and I, who were like brothers, because we were the same age, were really excited about this new development. Immediately we went to work. The evening started with lighting one cherry bomb at a time. Because our street was littered with empty beer bottles that were tossed carelessly aside by winos as they passed by, we decided to light the cherry bombs in the bottles and see if they would explode. To our satisfaction they did. After blowing up a few bottles, we got the ultimate idea. We made the decision to stuff as many empty bottles with cherry bombs and then squeeze as many of those bottles into the mailbox. After packing the mailbox with these makeshift bombs, we lit them, slammed the mailbox door closed and ran as fast and as far as we could. After a few moments we heard a tremendous boom! When we went to inspect the mailbox, it was completely disfigured. There were holes everywhere, the door was thrown violently across the street, and the blast was so intense that it blew our plastic mailbox right off the post! I dare not put into words how my mother responded.

The 3rd 'P' Of A High-Octane Church Is Preaching

The gospel causes explosions so intense that it mangles the kingdom of Satan and unhinges sin's power base. Paul in Romans 1:16 says, "For I am not ashamed of the gospel of Christ, for it is the power of God to salvation for everyone who believes." The word power comes from the Greek word *dynamis*, which is where we get the English word *dynamite*. God has put a stick of dynamite in our hands to obliterate any obstacle the enemy has put in humanity's path that would lead to eternal life. God knows that we cannot impose this type of carnage with a sparkler. Like dynamite, the gospel blows things up! When the gospel is unleashed, it leaves in its wake a race of people who have experienced the saving grace of God, sin's diminished stronghold on mankind, kindled flames of Christ's righteousness *(Romans 1:17)*, the recapturing of man's seat of affection and self-worth, and the restoration of God's image implanted in His creation.

Pentecost inaugurated an unprecedented season of courageous gospel preaching. That morning found 120 members of the Jerusalem church in unified earnest prayer. After the Spirit of God poured Himself on the church, the gospel was preached with clarity and when the dust settled, there were 3,000 people added to the church roll. I must point out that Peter was not alone preaching on that day. The Holy Spirit fell on everyone in the upper room *(Acts 2:2-3)*. Verse 4 iterates *"they were all filled with the Holy Spirit and began to speak with other tongues, as the Spirit gave them utterance."* Verse 11 gives the testimony of the multitude who had assembled in Jerusalem, *"we hear them speaking in our own tongues the wonderful works of God."* In a high-octane church, the preacher does not proclaim the gospel solely. Everyone is given a treasure chest of gospel dynamite. The gospel was detonated during Pentecost and 3000 individuals were extracted from the grip of death. Like my nephew and I ignited our cherry bombs on the 4th of July and shoved them in my mother's mailbox, God's people ignited their explosives on the day of Pentecost, shoved them into sin's abyss, and it was blown off of its foundation.

Set Off The Bomb

Every year, we stood waving the sparklers in a circular motion until the fire extinguished. This act was cute, but inconsequential. My mother gave us the sparklers because it was safe, and it did not cause any damage. The bomb, on the other hand, massacred the mailbox. The force of the blast left it devoid of further value. There was something that the sparkler and the cherry bomb had in common. They were both aroused with fire. However, the difference in the physical makeup of the sparkler and the cherry bomb determined how much damage they would inflict. The gospel contains capabilities that can annihilate anything in her path. It needs fire to unpack its destructive nature. Without the flame of preaching, the gospel is of none effect.

I pen this section with caution but at the same time with audacity. I do not want to offend anyone who reads this portion, but my mission to promote a high-octane church compels my audacious temperament. In future chapters we will deal with the importance of teaching, but for the purpose of this chapter, I must make a bold statement – The gospel was designed to be preached! If we look at our high-octane commission, you will notice that the first two parts specifically ask us to preach, whereas, the third part asks us to teach. Whenever the Bible discusses the presentation of the gospel, it always does so in the context of preaching. God designed the gospel to be transformational not informational.

When I was a student at Florida State University, all students received free tickets to go to the home football games. My reality was astronomically different in class than it was at a football game. In class, I sat, listened, recorded what the instructor had to say, and I took advantage of opportunities to ask questions. The interaction between the teacher and I was structured, limited, and designed to teach me something that I did not previously know. At the football game I was emotionally attached to the outcome of the football game. When FSU struggled, fell behind score wise, and eventually lost, I was tense, apprehensive, mad, and or sad. When my team performed well and eventually won, my mood was quite different. I was happy, overjoyed, and proud. I remember the electricity in our home stadium when it became apparent that FSU won the game. You could hear the boom of our roars and shouts as we cheered our team on. In class I had an intellectual interaction with my studies. At the football game I had an experiential interaction with the outcome of the game. I am not promoting emotionalism. I am advocating that preaching allows the hearer to experience the good news of Jesus Christ.

The Greek noun euangelion is translated as good news or gospel and has a rich history. When kings went to the battlefield for war, dispatched messengers would bring news to the citizens the king ruled over with the outcome of the battle. Sentinels would stand on top of the city walls awaiting the tidings of the messenger. The messenger would approach the city in a specific manner that would indicate if the king won or if he lost. If the messenger demonstrated that the king won, the sentinel would cry with a loud voice: Euangelion! Our King won! The inhabitants of the city had an emotional stake. If their king lost, they would be enslaved or destroyed by the opposing king. The citizens shouted just as they would have if they were on the battlefield with their king's army. The fact that our king won the battle should make us rejoice more than we would if we attended a football game and we watched our team vanquish our adversary.

Tailor Made

"The Spirit of the Lord is upon Me, because He has anointed Me to preach the gospel to the poor; He has sent me heal the brokenhearted, to proclaim liberty to the captives and recovery of sight to the blind, to set at liberty those who are oppressed; to proclaim the acceptable year of the Lord." (Luke 4:18) When we examine the ministry of Christ, it is easy to notice the clinical aspect of His miracles. He was a dermatologist, because He restored the leper's smoothness back to his skin. He was an ophthalmologist, because He restored the sight to the blind. He was a hematologist, because He cured the woman with the issue of blood. He was an orthoptist because He healed the paralytic. According to the text, Christ was anointed to preach, and the gospel was tailor made to address the spiritual, social, and sensational aspects of the human condition as well. God retrofitted the gospel to heal broken hearts, give liberty to the captives and the oppressed, counteract spiritual blindness, and offer hope for the future. The gospel paves a highway to salvation. This is precisely why the gospel is dynamite, because it blasts through rocks and structures that impede the progress of the sinner to have transformation. What good is a stick of dynamite if fire is absent to kindle it? What good is the gospel if the preacher is not available to thunder it from the mountain tops. As the inferno of preaching burns it ignites the dynamite of the gospel and shatters all obstacles in the way of the salvation of man.

Paul in his missive to the Roman church says, *"How then shall they call on him in whom they have not believed? And how shall they believe in him whom they have not heard? And how shall they hear without a preacher? And how shall they preach, except they be sent? As it is written, how beautiful are the feet of them that preach the gospel of peace and bring glad tidings of good things!" (Romans 10:14-15)* The gospel speaks through the medium of preaching.

The above passage presents dominoes that fall one by one. The domino that causes the other dominoes to fall is the preacher! When I was pursuing an M.A. in Pastoral Studies, one of my professors asked a question in class. He asked, "How does the gospel receive a hearing?" I am possibly oversimplifying the answer, but according to Romans 10:14, it is through preaching.

According to scripture, John the Baptist came, preaching (Matthew 3:1), Jesus came to Galilee preaching the gospel of the kingdom of God (Mark 1:14), The disciples preached everywhere (Mark 16:20), the apostles preached through Jesus the resurrection from the dead (Acts 4:2), and Jesus told us in the gospel commissions to preach (Mark 16:15; Luke 24:47).

Not The Pastor Only

A great and unfortunate misconception that exists in the body of Christ is that the preaching of the gospel can only be accomplished through the words and energy of the pastor. The pulpit stands as the pastor's greatest leadership tool, but the pulpit should not serve as a cage for the gospel. The gospel cannot be contained in the pulpit only. God designed the gospel to leak into the highways and the bi ways, the streets, and the mountain tops. Take a glimpse at the book of Acts where the prayer assembly mobilizes to pray in 1:13-14. One hundred and twenty people pack the upper room with their prayers and supplications. When the sound of the rushing mighty wind filled the house where they were praying, cloven tongues of fire sat upon each of them in 2:3. Verse 4 continues with the fact that they were all filled with the Holy Ghost and began to speak with other tongues as the Spirit gave them utterance. In verses 8 and 11, every man heard the wonderful works of

God in their own tongue. Up to this point, Peter had not stood to preach. The Gospel was preached by everyone who was endowed with the Spirit of God in the upper room. Allow your holy imagination to picture a moment where every member in your church goes looking together for the masses in the community and began to preach the wonderful works of God to the residents, and all the pastor has to do is extend the altar call like Peter did and give the invitation to repent, be baptized in the name of Jesus Christ, receive remission of sins, and accept the gift of the Holy Ghost (Acts 2:38). Picture the type of energy and heat that will generate and how the community will be impacted. Can you imagine what it will be like to claim entire street corners, blocks, neighborhoods, cities, countries, and continents for Christ through this intentional and aggressive form of evangelism that will literally turn the whole world upside down?

The world does not need another homiletician or another theologian. The world craves bold individuals who are unafraid to open their mouths and declare the magnificent good news of Jesus the Christ! God needs every hand-on-deck to accomplish the greatest commission ever given to humanity. Now is not the time to squabble over gender roles in the church, instead teach every man, woman, boy, and girl to preach the gospel. The most basic meaning of preaching is proclaiming. Everyone can proclaim the good news of Jesus Christ without a theological education. Just ask the Leper of Galilee (Mark 1:40-45), one of the ten lepers who was healed between Samaria and Galilee (Luke 17:11-19), the man healed by the pool of Bethesda (John 5:2-15) and ask the woman at the well (John 4). There was only one prerequisite that preceded the preaching of the gospel in all of the mentioned cases; each person experienced the goodness of Jesus Christ. Every church member experienced the gospel of Jesus Christ. If you have to, teach the congregation what they have experienced; teach them the gospel and empower them to proclaim it.

Choose a community and attack it with your army of believers like the 120 did on the day of Pentecost. Unleash each member to proclaim the gospel to everyone they encounter in the community. Publish the gospel house to house, apartment complex to apartment complex; go to parks, the recreation centers, grocery stores. Take the community by storm. Ask God for holy boldness and preach!

Summary
- The 3rd 'P' of a high-octane church is the preaching of the Gospel by every member.

> **What difference does it make for us to call ourselves Christians but never develop the habit of portraying Christ's attributes?**

CHAPTER 5

Just Like Your Daddy

"You act just like your daddy;" I heard on many occasions. As I grew older and began to matriculate through life, I went from just acting like my daddy to looking like my daddy. The fact that I am named after my father intensifies the situation. I look like my father, act like him, possess his name, and there are times when I am told that I walk like him. That means that my father photocopied himself when I was born. From what I understand, I started life resembling my mother and as I grew, my resemblance to my father became more profound and obvious. I now have two sons with the oldest having my name, which obviously belongs to my father as well. Many of his features are similar to my dad's. He is another photocopy of my dad.

The 4th 'P' Of A High-Octane Church Is Photocopy

Jesus told Nicodemus that he must be born again (John 3:3, 5). Originally, humanity bore the character of God. God fashioned us in His image; after His likeness (Genesis 1:26-27). Sin threw us down from our lofty estate and now our Godly resemblance has faded. Starting with the rebirth experience, Christ initiates our sanctification journey, and He photocopies Himself in us. Discipleship drives that process. One of the most vital programs every church must have is a robust discipleship program. Unfortunately, pastors and ministry leaders view discipleship as a way to instill denominational doctrines. Leaders also consider it as bible study. Mirroring Christ outweighs making someone a good member of a particular denomination. I am not discounting denominational teaching, but I am magnifying our Lord and Savior Jesus Christ. Discipleship is an intentional way to encourage the people of God to adopt His character. Christ does the work through the avenue of teaching. Sanctification is a divine work that Christ diligently performs. **"Being confident of this very thing, that he which hath begun a good work in you will perform it until the day of Jesus Christ." (Philippians 1:6)** God enlists men and women to reveal the divine character of God. Just like God empowers preachers to announce the gospel, He designates teachers to affirm His character. What difference does it make for us to call ourselves Christians but never develop the habit of portraying Christ's attributes? What sense does it make to establish a church if all our members do is show up for a weekend program and return home with the same deadly deficiencies, venomous vulnerabilities, wreckful weaknesses, and harmful habits? I want to take the time to draw a distinction. The good news of Jesus Christ must be shared with the world! We cannot afford the mistake of preaching the good news but neglect to learn how to live the good news. Through the Gospel, Christ converts humanity. Through discipleship, Christ clones Himself in humanity. **"Therefore, if any man be in Christ, he is a new creature: old things are passed away; behold, all things are become new." (2 Corinthians 5:17)**

Become Like Him

Jesus told Peter and Andrew in Matthew 4:19, ***"Follow me, and I will make you fishers of men."*** This was an invitation given by Jesus for us to come and follow Him and become His disciples. Verse 20 says, ***"At once they left their nets and followed Him."*** In verse 19 and 20, the word follow is used. The two 'follows' are two different Greek words with two separate meanings. In most situations when one thinks of following Christ, one thinks of walking behind Christ. This component is absolutely necessary, but the dynamics of the concept of discipleship is often missed when we think only from this view. In verse 19, the Greek word for follow is *duete*, which grammatically functions as an interjection in this passage. It literally means come! It served as a desperate overture on the part of Jesus for Peter and Andrew to follow Him. In verse 20 we see the response of Peter and Andrew which gives us insight into what discipleship is all about. The word 'follow' in verse twenty is akoloutheō in the Greek. This word expresses the concept of going the same way, not just in terms of going to the same destination but being united in character. In other words, akoloutheō expresses the idea that one follows to become just like the person who he/she follows. The whole point of discipleship is for us to become just like Jesus Christ. Discipleship is not just about teaching church doctrine. My father gave me his name, and I gave my son my name. I behave like my father and my son behaves like me. Christ gave us His name and over time we learn to behave like Him. Christ calls us not only to adopt His name and character, but we are called to replicate His name and His character in others. Discipleship equips us to function as Christ's protégés.

First Called Christians

Most of us know from experience how people watch and observe those of us who call ourselves Christians. We often hear indictments against Christianity in cases where professed Christians do not behave or handle situations according to who we promote Christ to be. We are under a tremendous microscope and we must always exemplify the character of Jesus Christ. The Antioch church was under such scrutiny in Acts 11:19-26. The scripture says in verse 26, **"and the disciples were first called Christians in Antioch."** Why were they called Christian in Antioch? To answer this question, we must get to the heart of what the word Christian means. In ancient times, the name Jesus was a common name in Israel, and it means Jehovah saves. The name Christ on the other hand possessed a more paramount implication. The name Christ comes from the Greek word *Christos* and it means 'the Anointed one.' When one investigates the miracles Jesus performed, there isn't any doubt that Jesus showed a consecration that was from on high. In addition, Christ was anointed at His baptism by the Holy Spirit *(Matthew 3:16)*. In Acts 11, the disciples were scattered after the persecution that arose over Stephen. Some of these disciples went to Antioch, preaching the Lord Jesus and the hand of the Lord was with them *(vs 21)*. The leaders in Jerusalem later sent Barnabas to Antioch. In verse 24, it was observed that Barnabas was full of the Holy Spirit and of faith. The citizens of Antioch witnessed that the disciples, along with Barnabas displayed an anointing similar to Christ's. Therefore, they were called *Christ-ians,* "the anointed ones." Illustrating the anointing of Christ is a part of the discipleship curriculum. Not only are we supposed to have His uprightness, but we are to have His unction. Jesus said Himself in John 14:12:

"Verily, verily, I say unto you, He that believeth on me, the works that I do shall he do also; and greater works than these shall he do; because I go unto my Father."

Make Disciples Of All Men

Christ was emphatic when He said *"Go ye therefore, and teach all nations, baptizing them in the name of the Father, and of the Son, and of the Holy Ghost." (Matthew 28:19)* Christ summoned us into partnership with Him in that we make the same call to the world that He made to us (Matthew 4:19-20; Matthew 28:19). Jesus commands us to make disciples of all men. This task is a required task and there is no way around it. We have the responsibility of duplicating ourselves by first becoming disciples and then making disciples of others. Notice, Christ says 'Go.' We do not wait for people to come to us, we initiate the process by going to the people. We go where people are located and we have a mandate to make them pupils of Christ: so that they can learn His words, His works, His ways. Paul says in 2 Corinthians 3:18: *"But we all, with open face beholding as in a glass the glory of the Lord, are changed into the same image from glory to glory, even as by the Spirit of the Lord."* The more sinners behold Christ, the more we become like Christ. By fulfilling the discipleship mandate, we are literally putting Christ's whole being on full display for the world to witness. The more we see the loveliness of His character, His wondrous works, and His majestic words, we become drawn to Him. Salvation is romantic and at times we believe that when we embrace Christ as our savior and king, it will be love at first sight. That may not always be the case, but discipleship will make Him more attractive, and our love for Him will intensify as the moments with Him go by.

The Curriculum

Christ handed us the discipleship curriculum on a silver platter. We usually miss something when we attempt to live out the commission found in Matthew 28. After Jesus tells us to make disciples of all men in verse 19, He tells us how to do it. According to verses 19 and 20:

a. Baptizing them in the name of the Father and the Son and the Holy Ghost.
b. Teaching them to observe all things that I have commanded you.

Baptism indicates that the sinner desires to turn away from their sins and receive the pardon of Jesus Christ (Acts 2:38). At the moment of baptism, we are disciples of Christ. Baptism is a part of the initial steps we take in our journey with Christ. Once that initial step is taken, another component activates so that the initial step leads to the end goal, which is to adopt the character of Christ; that step is teaching. Christ told us to teach. Back to Matthew 28:20. When we read this passage, we often miss what we are to teach. Most of us believe this is the moment that we teach new converts our doctrinal leanings. The word doctrine does mean teaching, and doctrines are important, but the question becomes' what do we teach to make one a disciple? Christ told us explicitly. We are to teach what He commanded. What did Jesus command? When we study the scriptures and the life of Christ, we discover that He issued 50 commandments during the life of His ministry. We were commanded to teach what Jesus commanded. Christ designed every commandment to show us how to live like Him. Notice, these are commandments. Christ commands His disciples to be like Him. He said that our righteousness must exceed the righteousness of the Pharisees, else, we are not worthy of the kingdom (Matthew 5:20). Christ's righteousness is exceptional and second to none. The righteousness that must resonate in His disciples belongs to Christ. Our righteousness the Bible tells us is as filthy rags (Isaiah 64:6). Christ imputes or delivers to us His righteousness as we are taught to be like Him.

The Next Step

God ignited an explosion on the day of Pentecost. The Holy Spirit filled the mouths of the 120 with the good news of Jesus Christ and their testimony penetrated the listening ears of the multitude. Peter summarized the gospel and made a call for repentance and baptism. Three thousand people courageously took their stand for Jesus and were baptized. Their journey did not stop there. The Bible says the 3000 continued steadfastly in the apostle's doctrine or teaching (Acts 2:42). Baptism did not secure the people in Christ; their dedication to learning more about Christ kept them energized and growing. After baptism, the next step is discipleship. After our old man is buried in the watery grave of baptism, Christ through discipleship is buried in the depths of our souls. We replicate the beauty of Christ in the world when people are intentionally discipled. As the church spreads her wings around the globe, she will be able to turn sinners into saints, while Christ photocopies Himself in the heart, mind, and soul of all believers.

Summary
- The 4th 'P' of a high-octane church is photocopy. She photocopies Christ in the life of every believer.

> **Jesus was famous for harnessing the power of fellowship.**

CHAPTER 6

All Hands On Deck

I dread Sundays! Saturdays are my busiest days and with each passing Saturday, I hope Sunday will allow me to recuperate from all the energy I exerted the previous day. It never works out that way. My family and I commute everywhere we go, because we live a good distance outside the city limits of Birmingham. My wife works in Birmingham. I work in Birmingham and Talladega. During the week, the window for my wife and children to leave the house and get to work and school on time is very small; which means that everything has to be in order ahead of time. We cannot afford to iron in the morning, so we iron the clothes for the week on Sundays. We plan the breakfast and snack schedules ahead of time as well. The mornings have to roll like a well-oiled machine; if not, my wife will be late for work. The prep work can be overwhelming for one individual to handle. All the clothes have to be washed, folded, and ironed. We stress to our kids the adage: 'many hands make the burden light.' All five members of our family engage in the process of making sure everything is in order so that the work and school week can flow as smoothly as possible. We work together because all of us benefit from the preparations that take place on Sunday. Barring any last-minute emergencies, the 'all hands-on-deck' approach allows us to get to our respective places on time.

The 5th 'P' of a High-Octane Church is Precincts

An often-overlooked mechanism functioned the same way in the early church. Acts 2:42 says, **"And they continued steadfastly in the apostles' doctrine and fellowship, in the breaking of bread, and in prayers."** Fellowship was an integral part of the culture of the early church. They continued steadfastly in fellowship. The fellowship that took place was more than just getting together. It was not a regular social event. It was much more than that. The word fellowship comes from the Greek word *koinōnia*. It means fellowship, participation, or partnership. The word grows from the concept of having things in common and these commonalities concerns everyone in the assembly. If we look to the instance when Peter was in prison, the scripture says: **"Peter was therefore kept in prison, but constant prayer was offered to God for him by the church." (Acts 12:5)** The church shared a common concern for Peter's well-being and freedom, so they gathered as a fellowship for an all-night prayer service at Mary's house (*Acts 12:12*). As a result of their earnest prayers an angel of the Lord was sent to release him from his jail cell.

The participation in fellowship was so contagious that Acts 4:32 says: **"Now the multitude of those who believed were on one heart and one soul; neither did anyone say that any of the things he possessed was his own, but they had all things in common."** The fellowship was concerned with the financial welfare of its members that those who owned lands and houses sold them and brought the proceeds to the apostle's feet to be distributed to anyone who had need *(Acts 4:34-35)*. This goes beyond going bowling together or having dinner at one another's homes; this is all about sharing similar concern for one another. The spiritual concerns of the group were also important to the fellowship and as a result, they met together to study the word of God and pray together (Acts 2:42).

People populate the church. The church is not a building, but a collection of individuals. The modern term 'community' comes from the same Greek word for fellowship: *'koinōnia.'* The church consists of community. She is a community of believers who have things in common. During my youth, my mother used to tell my siblings and I that all we had were one another. She said, "If I don't have, but you have, then by sharing, I have also." This notion captures the spirit of fellowship. Everyone participates in the spiritual, emotional, physical, psychological, and financial prosperity of every individual in the assembly. Within the fellowship, everyone has the 'all hands-on-deck' mentality.

Fellowship Multiplies The Church

When the lights are out at the church, when the sound equipment has been turned off, and every warm body has exited the building, the church goes dead; so, it appears. The church who has a strong fellowship culture, allows the force of the church to continuously advance forward. Participation in fellowship paves the way for a high-octane church. Take another look at Acts 2:42-47:

"And they continued steadfastly in the apostles' doctrine and fellowship, in the breaking of bread, and in prayers.

Then fear came upon every soul, and many wonders and signs were done through the apostles. Now all who believed were together, and had all things in common, and sold their possessions and goods, and divided them among all, as anyone had need. So, continuing daily with one accord in the temple, and breaking bread from house to house, they ate their food with gladness and simplicity of heart, praising God and having favor with all the people. And the Lord added to the church daily those who were being saved."

The church managed to grow everyday even outside of the divine service. The church was in operation mode twenty-four hours a day, seven days a week. The Lord added to the church daily. Remember the church is not a building; the church comprises of people. Also, the assembly did not have to be at the temple, synagogue, or church in order to grow. The context of the above passage takes place in fellowships: what we call small groups. Fellowships are church precincts that are setup so that the light of the church will never cease to burn. The Lord added to these precincts daily. How? These fellowships shared the same concerns, which included the salvation of mankind. Not only did they study and pray together. Not only did they divide their goods among each other. They also witnessed together; *"And daily in the temple, and in every house, they did not cease teaching and preaching Jesus as the Christ (Acts 5:42)."* Notice, every member was equipped to teach and preach Christ and the members joined forces to take care of this great work in their fellowship precincts. God added to these assemblies. The people who were joining the church did not necessarily walk down the aisle and take the preacher's hand. People made decisions for Christ in homes or wherever the fellowships gathered together.

Disregarding the fellowship represents one the greatest travesties of the church. The writer of Hebrews addresses how we can aggressively hold on to the hope that we profess. Each individual member becomes rooted and grounded in Christ through fellowship. The writer says: **"Let us hold fast the confession of our hope without wavering, for He who promised is faithful. And let us consider one another in order to stir up love and good works, not forsaking the assembling of ourselves together, as in the manner of some, but exhorting one another, and so much the more as you see the Day approaching." (Hebrews 10:23-25)** Most evangelists use this scripture to encourage consistent attendance at the weekly service, but the writer is really talking about fellowship overall; whether it is the weekend services or the small groups. The main point shows how love and good works can be stirred up in the hearts of every believer through fellowship. Unfortunately, we tend to form individual silos in the church, trying to take our journeys in Christ alone; 'Just me and Jesus!' One of the things I have observed in my pastoral ministry is that we have become comfortable just interacting with fellow church members only during Church services. Outside of the divine service, very few church members have any type of connection with one another. We are perfectly okay with living our lives separate from the assembly. As a matter of fact, many people do not want to have anything to do with the church outside of the allotted time for 'church service.' But when we get sick or if some type of calamity blindsides us, we are upset if no one from the church visits us and shows concern in those moments of crisis. Fellowship creates an environment where we are saturated with genuine love and concern at all times and in every facet of our lives.

Small group fellowship possesses a pastoral function. In the African American church, the pastor provides the majority of the pastoral care in a congregation. When people are ill and, in the hospital, they feel good when members from the church come to visit them. Ultimately, they want to see their pastor at their bedside. The fellowship can provide a pastoral care component that will be impossible for the pastors to handle for everyone in the congregation by themselves. If a member experiences any type of difficulty, he/she will automatically have a community of individuals who can rally around them and provide the oxygen they need so that they can continue to breathe spiritually. In a fellowship, there will be more than one person rolling up their sleeves to provide whatever the assistance is required to bridge the gap for the member going through crisis.

Jesus In Fellowship

Jesus was famous for harnessing the power of fellowship. Jesus called Levi the son of Alphaeus, who was also called Matthew, to follow Him (Mark 2:14). Jesus then goes to Levi's home to dine and many tax collectors and sinners also sat together with Jesus and His disciples (Mark 2:15). The Pharisees ask, how can Jesus eat and drink with tax collectors and sinners (Mark 2:16)? Jesus answers by saying in verse 17; ***"I did not come to call the righteous, but sinners, to repentance."*** Jesus saw fellowship as a method to call sinners to repentance. He capitalized on the opportunities that fellowship afforded in Luke 15. The Pharisees and scribes complained that Jesus received sinners and ate with them (Luke 15:2). He then articulates three different parables: the lost sheep, the lost coin, and the prodigal son. He rescues the lost sheep, He diligently searches for the lost coin, and He welcomes back the prodigal son. Notice in the last parable, Christ welcomes back the prodigal son even though the son who remained faithful and never left his father's side refused to attend the fellowship celebration that was in honor of the prodigal son. The father begged the faithful son to fellowship with his brother who had been lost. God is begging His church to show our faithfulness by investing whole-heartedly in fellowship. In these parables, Christ shows the efficacy of participating in fellowship. Through fellowship, we can attract those who are lost. By building upon the commonalities with those who may not have made up their minds to follow Christ will go a long way. Jesus never presented Himself as superior to anyone. He went where sinners were, He ate and fellowshipped with sinners. He never asked anyone to master a litmus test of 'do's and don'ts' in order to follow Him. Jesus presents Himself as someone who endures the same challenges that we face. He was tempted in all points as we are tempted (Hebrews 4:15).

Summary

- The 5th characteristic of a high-octane church are churches who have precincts (small groups) where strong fellowship takes place.

> **What we have, came as a result of God sharing with us and a byproduct of His generosity is that we have common ownership of what God owns.**

CHAPTER 7

What's Mine Is Yours

I still have a throbbing headache from some of the value systems that were pounded in my head in my developmental years. My mother would always tell my siblings and I: "If you don't have, but I have, then we all have." Unfortunately, we live in a society where materialism and individualism dominate the contours of our values. We subscribe to: "pull up your bootstraps," "the survival of the fittest," "every man for himself," and "don't just give a man a fish but teach him how to fish." We are taught to pursue our dreams at all cost and sacrifice to make them become a reality. On the surface these are worthy attributes for anyone to have, but if one is not careful, it can breed contempt for those who have not attained to the lofty goals that we have or has not shown the same level of ambition and motivation, or those seeking alms like the lame man by the gate Beautiful in Acts 3. God desires a Spirit of generosity to prevail among His people. The scripture says: **"Now all who believed were together, and had all things in common, and sold their possessions and goods, and divided them among all, as anyone had need." Acts 2:44-45**

All Things In Common

The Greek word for common is *koinos*. This Greek word packs a power punch that has been taken for granted by most church goers. The word expresses shared ownership. The modern Christian giver thinks about giving that lacks any resemblance to the high-octane church's system of giving found in Acts 2. The modern church hails a huge premium on what we call systematic giving. Yes, saying that I give God 10% of my increase sounds really good. If we look at it from God's perspective, I believe our thinking on giving will be altered forever. The Bible teaches that God owns everything. **"The earth is the Lord's, and all its fullness, the world and those who dwell therein" (Psalm 24:1; NKJV).** What we have, came as a result of God sharing with us and a byproduct of His generosity is that we have common ownership of what God owns. When we give our tithe, we are acknowledging that what we own is owned by God at the same time. The high-octane church embodies this enigma. Giving goes beyond what I put in the offering plate from week to week. Rather, giving now promotes a unique mindset of shared ownership. What's mine is yours.

The 6th 'P' Of A High-Octane Church Is Philanthropy

There is a second sense to this power-punched Greek word. It also communicates the idea that the community of faith were participants in each other's plight. Through the vehicle of philanthropy, the rich share in the circumstance of the poor and the poor in the circumstance of the rich. John 1:14, says that Jesus pitched His tent among us. Christ went a step further in that, **"He made Himself of no reputation, taking the form** *of a bondservant, and coming in the likeness of men. And being found in appearance as a man, He humbled Himself and became obedient to the point of death, even the death of the cross." (Philippians 2:7-8)* Christ took on our poverty so that we could experience His prosperity, our sin so we could receive His salvation, and our bondage so we could share in His birthright. When united with Christ, we have all things in common. Christ became poor and destitute as we are, and we become rich and wealthy as Christ is. He dies our death so we could live His life. Charity puts us on the same plane with our sisters and brothers. When we give, our siblings in Christ share in our abundance, and in turn we have an opportunity to walk in their shoes by tasting their aridity. Philanthropy brings us together and allows us to experience true fellowship and comradery. Equality prevails because we both have the same lack and liquidity at the same time. **"Now all who believed were together and had all things in common." Acts 2:45.**

The Generosity Of God

The scripture portrays God as the most generous person in the history of humanity. The philanthropy of salvation serves as a model for the high-octane church. God shared His most precious commodity with humanity. *"For God so loved the world that He gave His only begotten Son, that whoever believes in Him should not perish but have everlasting life." (John 3:16)* God did not give us out of His abundance, but rather out of His scarcity; for Jesus was God's only begotten Son. We can go a step further with this concept. The Greek word for *gave* is *didōmi* and it really expresses the spirit of philanthropy that God demonstrated to humanity, because the word implies that

Jesus was donated by God to humanity. God did not dispense a percentage of His prized possession, instead He gave us all. God designed salvation to embody a transaction. God gave us Jesus and in return, we Give Him our heart. One can argue that when God captures our heart, He has shared ownership of our hearts. Therefore, the question: Where is your treasure? Jesus said in Matthew 6:21: **"For where your treasure is, there your heart will be also."** This transactional generosity demonstrates that God has placed His treasure on this earth, while we are to place our treasure in Heaven. The divine axiom can be understood this way: Because the Father's treasure has been placed on planet earth in the person of Jesus, we therefore share the Father's heart. In turn, when we place our treasure in heaven, God has permission to share our heart.

Excessive Giving

The Old Testament stressed a systematic giving system. A tenth was required for tithe along with a liberal offering. The people gave up to one-third of their increase. As a result of the Pentecostal experience we witness in Acts 2, God outpoured the spirit of generosity upon the inhabitants of the upper room and it was infectious and contagious. It was no longer enough to calculate percentages to be given, rather, their heart for giving became such a phenomenon that the Bible notes: **"and sold their possessions and goods, and divided them among all, as anyone had need." Acts 2:45.** Acts 4:34 indicates that no one had any lack. The United States has a welfare system that provides resources and services to the least among us, but the early church installed a welfare system on steroids. The needs of the people were provided for within the walls of the church. I truly believe God had this in mind in the old covenant when He says in Malachi 3:10; **"Bring all the tithes into the storehouse, that there may be food in My house, and try Me now in this, says the Lord of hosts, "If I will not open for you the windows of heaven and pour out for you such blessing that there will not be room enough to receive it." (NKJV)**

The amazing fact of this outcome of such divine philanthropy was that the generous givers did not sustain any lack themselves. By mimicking Malachi 3:10 and laying what they sold at the Apostles' feet, they truly experienced the overabundant blessings of God. By far, philanthropy may show overwhelming evidence that the Holy Spirit works as the dominant force in the high-octane church. Philanthropy puts a value on love for others and devalues the love of self. Jesus did say **"By this all will know that you are My disciples, if you have love for one another." John 13:35 (NKJV)**

Don't Hold Back

Acts 5 gives one of the most brutal realities of what happens when we are not as generous as we could be. Ananias and his wife Sapphira were possibly inspired by the philanthropy of Joses, surnamed Barnabas who had land, sold it, and brought the money and laid it at the apostles' feet (Acts 4:36-37). They decided to do the same. When it was time to truly demonstrate the spirit of generosity, they conspired to hold back some of the proceeds from the sale of their land (Acts 5:2). Peter who interrogated them about their decision indicated that they did not lie to men, but rather to God. **"Then Ananias, hearing these words, fell down and breathed his last." (Acts 5:5a)** Death takes place when we withhold our generosity from God and the body of Christ. Ananias and Sapphira possessed the resources to perpetuate the vibrancy of the church and feed her ability to thrive, but they held back their philanthropy. They put more value on their personal prosperity over the prosperity of the body of Christ. Therefore, they died. Compassion, love, and generosity dies in us when we decide to selfishly indulge our selfish behaviors. Ananias and Sapphira robbed those who were less fortunate to experience their prosperity, and in turn Ananias and Sapphira were robbed of the opportunity to share in the life of less fortune.

Summary
- The 6th characteristic of a high-octane church are churches who have a prevalent spirit of philanthropy.

CHAPTER 8

What They Don't Say

My Grandmother used to say< "Don't pay attention to what people say, but what they do not say." So much could be said of what we leave unsaid. What have we failed to say about Jesus? We should publish good, exciting, and wonderful things about God from the mountaintop. Jonah Berger in his book *Contagious: Why Things Catch On,* says: "Word of mouth is more effective than traditional advertising." Just like any product, the church's positive popularity depends on constructive feedback from others. Marketing platforms saturate the marketplace and there are many niches available to churches and leaders. If not careful, we can fall into the pit of marketing campaigns that highlight our programs, ministries, enthusiasm, and relevance as the main product, instead of launching a campaign which publishes glad tidings about God. God has to be the focal point of any marketing effort. The scripture says: *"And continuing daily with one mind in the temple, and breaking bread from house to house, they ate their food with gladness and simplicity of heart, praising God and having favor with all the people. And the Lord added to the church daily those who were being saved."* (Acts 2:46-47)

The 7th 'P' Of A High-Octane Church Is Praise

The Greek word for praise is *aineō*, which expresses the idea of "speaking well of." We have a duty as disciples to speak well of God. During the triumphant descent of the Mount of Olives, **"the whole crowd of the disciples began to rejoice and praise God with loud voices *for all the mighty works that they had seen...*" (Luke 19:37).** With unashamed, unfiltered, and unrestrained loud voices, the disciples spoke well of God because of the works they witnessed Jesus perform. As the Pharisees looked on with scrutiny upon the crowd of disciples, they said to Jesus, **"Teacher, rebuke your disciples."** (vs. 39). He answered them, **"I tell you, if these should be silent, the stones would immediately cry out."** (vs. 40). God must receive praise! The praise might as well come from the mouth of His disciples, otherwise, the rocks will do it for us. We normally think of praise in the context of a worship service. Consider the clamoring noise of praise that broke forth as Jesus entered into Jerusalem riding on a white donkey. It was not during an official worship time, rather, the people spontaneously began to speak well of God as they witnessed Jesus who performed so many miracles, make His way into the city. Just the sight and presence of Jesus ignited a response of testimony and praise reports.

Praise More Valuable Than Money

Acts 3 begins with Peter and John on a collision course with a man who was lame from his mother's womb during the hour of prayer. The lame man saw these two men and asked for alms. Peter answered by saying, **"Silver and gold I do not have, but what I do have I give you: In the name of Jesus Christ of**

Nazareth, rise up and walk" *(vs. 6)*. A budget line item was not available to Peter and John for marketing. The only currency available to them was the name of Jesus. Look what happens next! "So, he leaping up, stood and walked and entered the temple with them – walking, leaping, and praising God. There goes that word praise again! Suddenly, the man who now is a former lame man, became magnetized because of his praise. He was speaking well of God and attributing his transformation from a lame man to a walking and leaping man. **"Now as the lame man who was healed held on to Peter and John, all the people ran together to them in the porch which is called Solomon's, greatly amazed."** What attracted the people to run to Peter and John was the lame man's praise. No matter the size of our marketing budgets, the sophistication of the media platforms, the expertise of industry leaders, whether or not a consultant is hired, if we have a marketing team, the brightness, the glare of our church operation; Praise, our speaking well of God, will ultimately draw others to Christ. The Psalmist said: **"So we, Your people and sheep of your pasture, will give You thanks forever; we will show forth Your praise to all generations."** (Psalm 79:13)

Spread The Word

Jesus benefited from the muscle-flexing testimonies of key people, who spoke highly of Him. John 1:29-36 chronicles the testimony of John the baptizer. He said that Jesus was preferred above him, he saw the Spirit descending from heaven like a dove, and remained upon Him, testified that He was the Son of God, and called Him the Lamb of God. Two of John's disciples who heard John's testimony followed Jesus. One of the two disciples was Andrew and he went to his brother Simon and said to him, "We have found the Messiah" and brought him to Jesus. The following day, Jesus found Philip and beckoned him to follow Him. Phillip found Nathanael and said to him, "We have found Him of whom Moses in the law, and also the prophets, wrote – Jesus of Nazareth, the son of Joseph." John spoke well of Jesus in the hearing of two of his disciples. Andrew one of the two disciples spoke well of Jesus to his brother Simon. Philip spoke well of Jesus to Nathanael. We are commissioned to spread the word and share with others who we have found. The church must unleash her praise of God. She must speak well of her savior. The church cannot reserve her praise for the worship service only. We must speak well of God on the mountain top, in the valley low, on the street corner, in the break room, on the phone, using our social media platforms, in our advertisements. Praise Him! Praise Him! Praise Him!

Summary
- The 7th characteristic of a high-octane church are churches who are willing to praise God!

CHAPTER 9

Value Added

"A good name is to be more desired than great wealth, favor is better than silver and gold." The Christian church has absorbed a devastating blow to her reputation. It used to mean something to call oneself a Christian. This book has not been structured to really speak to all the various reasons why it is no longer the church's reality. Unfortunately, dormant ministries, dying congregations, deteriorating buildings, determined unwillingness to change, and dynamic religious alternatives litter the modern landscape. The scripture says: "praising God and having favor with all the people. And the Lord added to the church daily those who were being saved." Acts 2:47. The Greek word for favor is delight or joyful. The people were delighted by the presence of this new phenomenon called the church.

Added Value To The Community
Many churches have some form of community service thrust, program, or ministry. The church gives out food, pays rent and utilities, mentors and tutors children, assists single mothers, ministers to the homeless community, hosts job fairs, encourages health and wellness, advocates for economic

empowerment, tackles social injustices, and we can add many other items to the list. I believe to my core that these things are necessary and commendable. As an endeavoring high-octane church, I believe we have to travel farther. When we look at the early church, there was a particular value they added to the surrounding Jerusalem community: they added the transferred power of Jesus the Messiah. The church became the conduit of the goodness, generosity, glory, and the grandeur of Jesus. If we survey the entire book of Acts and consider the side effect the day of Pentecost had on the people, we will see the value that Jesus added to the people that was unquantifiable.

- Acts 3 – Lame man healed in the name of Jesus
- Acts 5 – Multitudes were healed, and unclean spirits cast out
- Acts 8 – City of Samaria receives Christ & Ethiopian converted to Christ
- Acts 9 – The unlikely conversion of Saul
- Acts 10 – Spirit falls on Gentiles beginning with Cornelius and his household
- Acts 11 – Gospel spreads its tentacles to the world

If we were to go back to Acts 3:1-7, we see a template for how we should view community service and how this service impacts our reputation. "Now Peter and John went up together to the temple at the hour of prayer, the ninth hour. And a certain man lame from his mother's womb was carried, whom they laid daily at the gate of the temple which is called Beautiful to ask alms from those who entered the temple; who, seeing Peter and John about to go into the temple, asked for alms. And fixing his eyes on him, with John, Peter said, 'Look at us.' So, he gave them his attention, expecting to receive something from them. Then Peter said, 'Silver and gold I do not have, but what I do have I give you: In the name of Jesus Christ of Nazareth, rise up and walk.'" Notice a man who is positioned outside the church is lame and asking for alms (community service) of everyone who is walking inside. I am sure there were other worshipers, who arrived before Peter and John that gave the lame man alms. They gave alms, but the alms did not change the lame man's condition. When Peter and John arrived, he was still lame. Peter and John do something revolutionary. They did not give money; "Silver and gold I do not have." What they gave instead was more valuable than money, alms, feeding programs, job fairs, economic empowerment, etc. "But what I do have I give you: In the name of Jesus Christ of Nazareth, rise up and walk." Peter and John gave the lame man the transferred power of Jesus which changed his life. He was no longer lame, which factored into his having to ask for alms. The value that Jesus added was more than what Peter and John could have put in the lame man's jar. I am not saying that the church should not provide the various community services, programs, and initiatives; rather I am saying that Jesus adds more value to the life of the community.

The church should not be known primarily as an institution that provide various generous services. The community and the world should recognize the church as a body of believers that possess the transferred power of Jesus.

"So he, leaping up, stood and walked and entered the temple with them – walking, leaping, and praising God. And all the people saw him walking and praising God (Acts 3:8-9)." This man's experience with the power of Jesus, led him to

praise God and became the catalyst behind an additional five thousand men believing on Jesus. (Acts 4:4)

The Value That Jesus Added

"The Spirit of the Lord is upon Me, because He has anointed Me to preach the gospel to the poor; He has sent Me to heal the brokenhearted, to proclaim liberty to the captives and recovery of sight to the blind, to set at liberty those who are oppressed; to proclaim the acceptable year of the Lord." (Luke 4:18-19)

Community	Value
Poor	Gospel
Brokenhearted	Healing
Captives	Liberty
Blind	Recovery of Sight
Oppressed	Liberty

All the value that was added in the above table is wrapped in the person of Jesus Christ. If the value of Christ is shared with our community, then the church will be able to add value to the lives of the poor, brokenhearted, captives, blind, and the oppressed. The church will have the reputation of having the transferred value of the power of Jesus.

About The Author

Jacques Francois is a pastor who has endured the high and lows of ministry. He is the husband of a school teacher, and father to three wonderful children. He has been a radio personality and contributed articles in Ministry Magazine. Pastor Francois and his family call Louisville home where he pastors the New Life SDA Church.

www.ingramcontent.com/pod-product-compliance
Lightning Source LLC
Chambersburg PA
CBHW052104110526
44591CB00013B/2343